SCHOLASTIC

CREATING SMART BOARD™ LESSONS Yes, You Can!

Easy Step-by-Step Directions for Using SMART Notebook Software to Develop Powerful, Interactive Lessons That Motivate All Students

Marcia Jeans

New York • Toronto • London • Auckland • Sydney
Mexico City • New Delhi • Hong Kong • Buenos Aires

Teaching *Resources*

NOTE: The instructions in this book are designed for Windows-based computers. Mac users will find the majority of the directions will apply with a few differences.

Editor: Maria L. Chang

Cover design by Jorge J. Namerow

Interior design by Holly Grundon

ISBN: 978-0-545-22134-4

Table of **Contents**

Introduction 4

Understanding How Your SMART Board Works 6

Orienting Your SMART Board 7

SMART Notebook Software 7

Part 1:
SMART Notebook Basics

Navigation Tips 10

Typing Text 13

Pen Tools 14

Shapes and Lines Tools 18

The Gallery 20

Locking Down Objects 23

Grouping and Layering Objects 24

Cloning 26

Screen Shade 28

Dual Page Display 29

Tables 31

Saving, Printing, and Exporting 37

Part 2:
Beyond the Basics

Customizing Tools 40

Hyperlinks 45

Animation 50

Screen Capture Tools 51

Adding Graphics 55

My Content 58

Importing Files 63

Floating Tools Toolbar 66

Ink Aware 69

Part 3:
Create Your Own Lessons

Math: Find the Area 71

Language Arts: Spin a Plural 74

Science: Name That Animal! 76

Appendix: Professional Resources 78

Introduction

Chances are, if you are reading this book, you already have a SMART Board™ in your classroom or expect to have one very soon. And like many other teachers, you're probably not quite sure how to make the most of this electronic board that looks deceptively familiar, yet is obviously far more high tech than a regular whiteboard. Not to worry! This book, *Creating SMART Board Lessons: Yes, You Can!* is designed to help you master the various tools and features of the SMART Board so that you can take full advantage of this interactive teaching device to enhance your day-to-day lessons.

Interactive whiteboards are increasingly becoming commonplace in classrooms all over the globe, especially in the United States. According to America's Digital Schools 2008 report, 85 percent of school districts in the United States use interactive whiteboards. More than half of those whiteboards are SMART Boards. There are several great reasons for using interactive whiteboards in the classroom. In its report "What the Research Says About Interactive Whiteboards" (Coventry, 2003), the British Educational Communications and Technology Agency detailed the benefits students received from using the interactive whiteboard in the classroom:

- increased enjoyment and motivation

- greater opportunities for participation and collaboration

- improved personal and social skills

- ability to cope with more complex concepts

- accommodation for different learning styles

- increased self confidence

In addition, a study by Marzano and Haystead (2009) indicated that using interactive whiteboards to teach lessons resulted in a 16 percentile point gain in student achievement. Furthermore, because interactive whiteboards offer different ways to engage with content—tactile, visual, and auditory— students with learning disabilities seem to benefit the most.

At the heart of the SMART Board is the SMART Notebook software, which makes it possible for teachers to create engaging, content-rich lessons that address specific student skills. This book contains step-by-step directions and resources to help you master the essentials of SMART Notebook software. Included with the book is a DVD that contains instructional videos, hands-on practice pages, and sample Notebook lessons. By the time you finish this book, you will find yourself creating and including more digital and interactive content into your lessons on a regular basis. With a SMART Board as your teaching partner, you can:

- teach whole-class lessons

- introduce and drum up excitement about a new concept

- model an activity before having students do them independently

- review content at the end of a unit

- show videos to support a lesson

- manipulate text and objects on screen

- write, save, and print lesson notes for students

- encourage active, hands-on participation

- and so much more!

Ready to get the most of your SMART Board? Then let's get started!

References

British Educational Communications and Technology Agency (BECTA). (2003). "What the Research Says About Interactive Whiteboards." Coventry, U.K.: ICT Research.

Greaves, T. W., & Hayes, J. (2008). *America's Digital Schools 2008*. Shelton, CT: MDR.

Marzano, R. J., & Haystead, M. (2009). *Final report on the evaluation of the Promethean technology*. Englewood, CO: Marzano Research Laboratory.

Understanding How Your SMART Board Works

First, let's take a glimpse at how the SMART Board works:

The projector and the SMART Board are connected to a computer. Through the projector, an image of the computer screen is displayed on the SMART Board. The SMART Board then takes it a step further and acts as an interactive touch-screen monitor for the computer. By touching the SMART Board, you can open applications, write or draw with digital ink, save your notes and lessons, and much more. Once you have learned all the advantages and features of your SMART Board, you will never use a regular whiteboard or an overhead projector again!

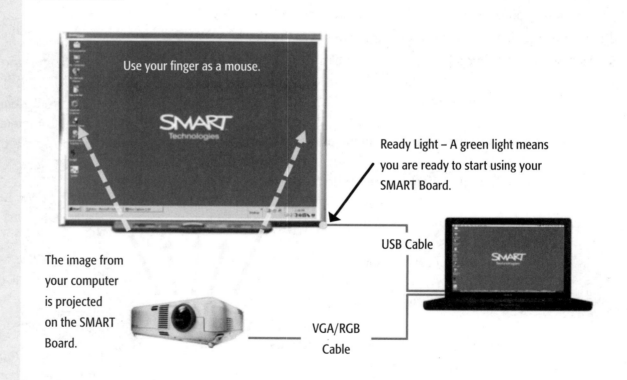

Use your finger as a mouse.

Ready Light – A green light means you are ready to start using your SMART Board.

USB Cable

The image from your computer is projected on the SMART Board.

VGA/RGB Cable

Tip:

If you ever need assistance with setting up your SMART Board, don't hesitate to contact SMART Technologies technical support. Visit their Web site at http://smarttech.com for information on how to contact their technical support department.

Orienting Your SMART Board

After hooking up your SMART Board to your computer and projector, you will need to orient the board. Orienting the board helps provide a precise response to a finger or Pen Tool touch. There are many different ways to orient the SMART Board. The easiest and quickest way is to click the two buttons on the Pen Tray at the bottom of the SMART Board. Once clicked, a screen will appear with nine (or more, depending on the size of your SMART Board) spots on the board for you to touch and orient the board.

Press both buttons at the same time to begin the orienting process.

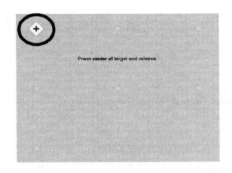

Begin the orienting process at the upper-left corner of the Orientation screen. Press your finger or pen firmly on the center of each cross in the order indicated by the white, diamond-shaped icon.

Tip:

If you are not satisfied with the precision of a particular orientation point while orienting, press one of the Pen Tray buttons or the left arrow key on your keyboard to redo the previous orientation point.

SMART Notebook Software

SMART Notebook is a feature-rich, dynamic software application that comes with your SMART Board. It enables you to create interactive and exciting lessons. This software comes with a multitude of digital resources that include pictures, clip art and diagrams, backgrounds, dynamic Flash files, word games, quizzes, and video/audio files. From an interactive hundred chart to a simulation that shows the relationship of time, distance, and speed, SMART Notebook has the resources to enhance instruction for every subject and grade level.

When you purchase a SMART Board, the software will be shipped along with the board. However, it is always best to download the software from the SMART Technologies Web site (http://smarttech.com) to ensure you have the latest version of the software. SMART updates Notebook software on a regular basis, and you will want the latest and greatest. To download the software, you will need the SMART Board's serial number, which is located in two places: on the back of your SMART Board interactive whiteboard and on the front or side of the bottom-right corner of the frame, as indicated in the diagram below.

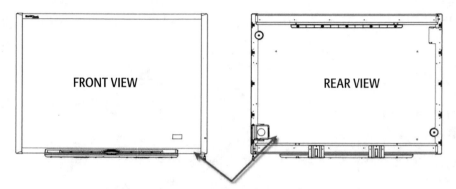

Serial Number Locations: The serial number on your SMART Board interactive whiteboard always begins with the letters *SB*, followed by the interactive whiteboard's model number.

Keep Updated

If you already have SMART Notebook on your computer, keep it updated for free! To see if any updates are available, go to the menu bar and click on *Help > Check for Updates*.

A new window will appear and, if any components of your software needs updating, click on the Update button.

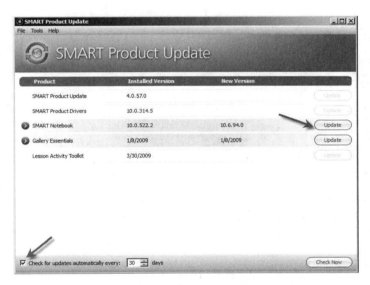

SMART Notebook components that need updating will be highlighted. Click the Update button to start the process.

Want a reminder to check for software updates? Make sure this button is checked.

PART 1
SMART Notebook Basics

Using the SMART Notebook software, you can create highly engaging, interactive lessons and activities that include dynamic text, graphics, shapes, tables, and so much more. This section will show you how to get started by opening the software, adding text to your pages using a variety of fonts, utilizing the different pen tools, creating and manipulating shapes and lines, and more. You'll also learn about useful features, such as the Gallery, cloning, screen shade, dual screen display, and others. Don't forget to check out the bonus DVD for video clips and practice Notebook pages for extra help!

Navigation Tips

Navigating SMART Notebook software is a snap. This section will show you how to open the software and help you find your way around.

SMART Notebook software can be opened in a variety of ways:

1   Click on the Notebook Software icon on your desktop.

Notebook
Software 10

OR

Watch the DVD

On the enclosed DVD, you'll find helpful tutorials, both in video and Notebook formats. To access the videos, click on **Creating SMART Board Lessons.pdf**. This will launch a menu with links to the various video tutorials. (You'll need Adobe Reader 9.0 or higher. You can download it for free at http://get.adobe.com/reader.) To access the Notebook file, click on **Practicing SMART Skills.notebook**.

2 Click on *Start > All Programs > SMART Technologies > Notebook Software > Notebook Software 10*

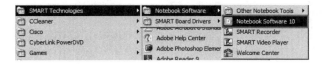

OR

3 Click on the SMART Board icon on your system tray and then select *Notebook*.

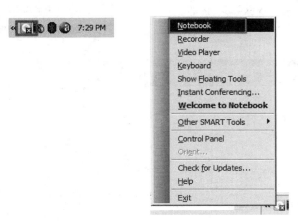

When you first open Notebook software, you will be taken to the Welcome Center. The SMART Welcome Center provides access to many of the tools, resources, and files you can use with your SMART Board.

Open a new Notebook file.

Find your recently opened Notebook files here.

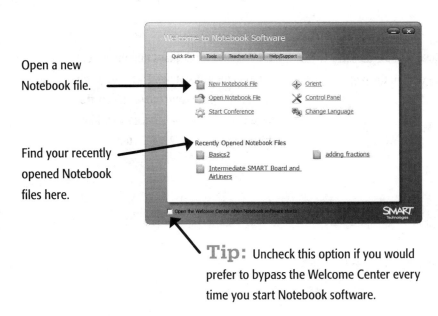

Tip: Uncheck this option if you would prefer to bypass the Welcome Center every time you start Notebook software.

When you open a new Notebook file, you will see a blank page. You can add as many pages as you want to your file. Add a new page by clicking on the Add New Page icon on the toolbar in the top left-hand corner. Navigate back and forth between pages by using the blue arrows or by using the Page Sorter. The toolbars on the top and on the left can easily be moved to the bottom or to the right.

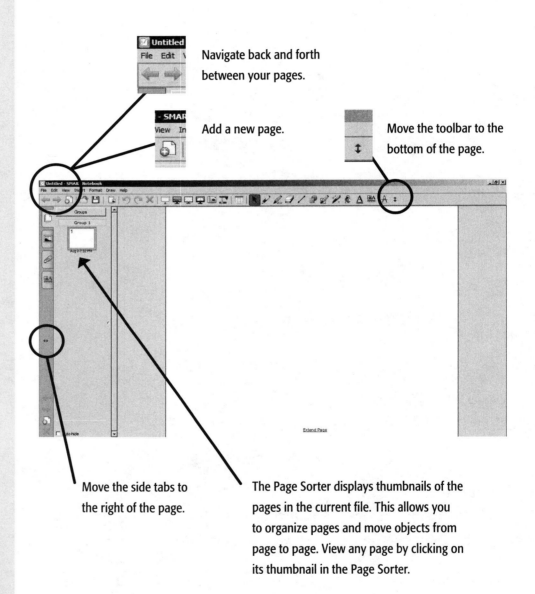

Navigate back and forth between your pages.

Add a new page.

Move the toolbar to the bottom of the page.

Move the side tabs to the right of the page.

The Page Sorter displays thumbnails of the pages in the current file. This allows you to organize pages and move objects from page to page. View any page by clicking on its thumbnail in the Page Sorter.

Watch the DVD

Want to learn more tips on how to navigate in SMART Notebook? Watch "Navigation Tips" on the DVD.

Typing Text

In order to create your own amazing Notebook lessons, you will need to know how to add text to your pages. This section shows you how simple it is to do.

To type text on a page, simply begin typing on the page with your computer keyboard. A textbox is automatically created as you type and the Font toolbar appears. To change font type, color, or size, highlight the text and make your selections on the toolbar.

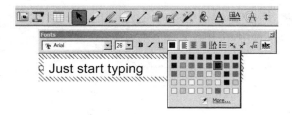

Once you are finished typing, click on the Select arrow.

Now you can move your typed text anywhere on the page. Simply drag the text to the desired location. (Text will not move if you are editing the text and the Fonts toolbar is showing.)

Drag this text to any location on the page.
Just click and drag.

You can also resize your text by clicking *once* on the textbox, clicking the resize handle (the white circle), and then dragging it to increase or reduce the object's size.

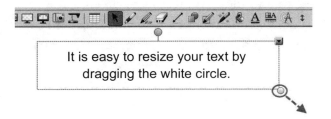

It is easy to resize your text by dragging the white circle.

Tip:

SMART Notebook automatically checks spelling as you type text on a page. Misspelled words are underlined (just like in other word-processing programs). Just remember, the misspelled words will be marked only when you are editing the textbox. Right-click on a misspelled word to get suggested spellings.

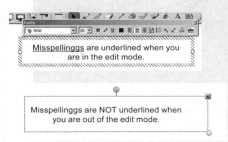

Misspellinggs are underlined when you are in the edit mode.

Misspellinggs are NOT underlined when you are out of the edit mode.

Watch the DVD

Want to learn more tips on how to type text in SMART Notebook? Watch "Typing Text" on the DVD.

If you ever need to edit your text, just double-click on the textbox and make the desired changes.

Hands-on Practice

Ready to give your new Notebook skills a try? Open the *Practicing SMART Skills.notebook* file and click on the arrow next to "Typing, Editing, and Changing Text."

Pen Tools

Your SMART Board has four pens in the Pen Tray, but SMART Notebook software has an even wider variety of pens that you can utilize. Let your creativity run wild!

There are four types of pens in SMART Notebook software.

 Pens – This basic tool has six colors of pens and two highlighters, all of which can be customized (see pages 41–42).

 Creative Pens – If you want to add colorful elements to your presentations, you can draw freehand objects using the Creative Pens. The Creative Pens enable you to draw a line of rainbow colors, smiley faces, stars, and more.

Shape Recognition Pen – You can use the Shape Recognition Pen to draw circles, ovals, squares, rectangles, triangles, and arcs.

 Magic Pen – With this tool, you can create a spotlight, magnification area, or fading text.

Pens

Once you click on the Pens tool, you can select from a variety of pen types, colors, and sizes. The last two selections are highlighters. Simply start writing or drawing on the page. To remove the pen marks, you can click on them and press the Delete key on your keyboard or use the Eraser tool. (You will learn later in this book how to customize the pens.)

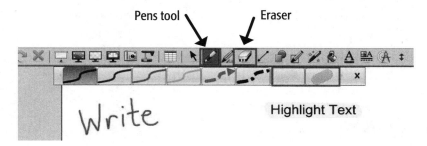

Creative Pens

The Creative Pens tool gives you access to different "ink" types. After selecting the ink type, simply start writing or drawing on the page. To remove the pen marks, you can click on them and press the Delete key on your keyboard or use the Eraser tool. The Creative Pens are not customizable.

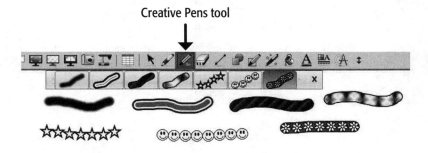

Some examples of SMART Notebook's Creative Pens

Shape Recognition Pen

Click on the Shape Recognition Pen to start drawing a shape. If SMART Notebook recognizes your drawing as a circle, oval, square, rectangle, triangle, or arc, it will automatically replace the shape on the page. The Eraser tool doesn't remove shapes. To delete a shape, simply click on it and press the Delete key on your keyboard or use the menu arrow of the shape and select *Delete* from the list of options.

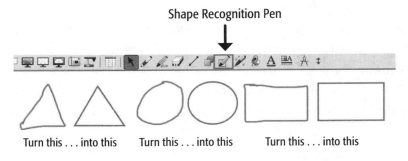

Shape Recognition Pen

Turn this . . . into this   Turn this . . . into this   Turn this . . . into this

Great for creating graphic organizers and teaching math!

Magic Pen

The Magic Pen performs three main functions, depending on how you use it. To create a **spotlight**, simply draw a circle or oval on the page after selecting the Magic Pen. A spotlight will appear while the rest of the page darkens. This spotlight can be moved and resized. A great tool for bringing attention to part of a page!

Draw a circle for the spotlight to magically appear!

Close the spotlight by clicking on the X.

Move the spotlight around the page by dragging in any direction.

Watch the DVD

Want to see the Magic Pen in action? Watch "Magic Pen" on the DVD.

To create a **magnifier**, simply draw a rectangle on the page with the Magic Pen. The area inside the rectangle will now be magnified.

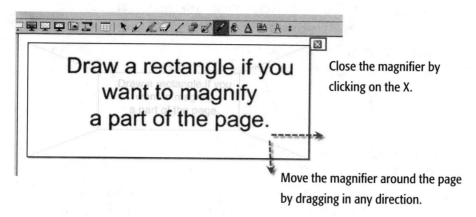

Close the magnifier by clicking on the X.

Move the magnifier around the page by dragging in any direction.

To create **fading text**, start writing with the Magic Pen. The ink will automatically disappear in a few seconds.

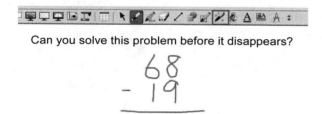

Can you solve this problem before it disappears?

$$68 \\ - 19$$

Tip:

Be careful when writing the number zero or the letter O with the Magic Pen. The tool will think you want to add a spotlight! A solution to this problem is to create your letter or number like this.

Tip:

Whenever you use a tool from the toolbar, always return to the Select tool when you are finished!

Select tool

Shapes and Lines Tools

You can use the Shapes tool to create a variety of shapes, including geometric shapes, check marks, an X, and more. With the Lines tool, you can draw straight lines, line segments, and more.

Shapes Tool

To access the Shapes tool, click on the Shapes icon on the toolbar. A variety of shapes will be displayed. After selecting a shape, press where you want to place the shape on the page and drag until the shape is the size you want. You can create perfect circles, squares, triangles, and other shapes by holding down the Shift key as you draw the shape.

Shapes tool

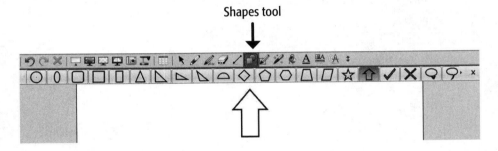

Select the desired shape. Press where you want the shape to go on the page and drag to the desired size.

You can drag the shape to any location on the page.

To rotate the shape, press the object's rotation handle (the green circle), and then drag it in the direction you want to rotate the shape.

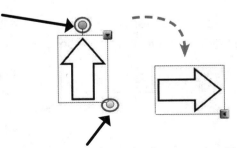

To change its size, press the object's resize handle (the white circle), and then drag it to increase or reduce the shape's size.

To delete a shape from a page, select the shape and choose **Delete** from the menu arrow. You can also press the Delete key on your keyboard or use the red X on the toolbar.

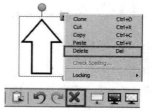

Lines Tool

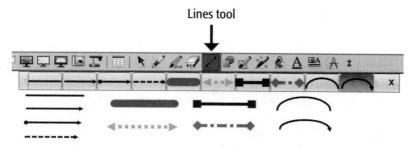

To access the Lines tool, click on the Lines icon on the toolbar. A selection of line styles will appear below the toolbar. After selecting a line style, press where you want to place the line on the page and drag until the line is the length you want.

A variety of lines are available in SMART Notebook. Use them to create graphic organizers, rays, angles, T-charts, and more.

You can drag the line to any location on the page. To rotate the line, press the object's rotation handle (the green circle), and then drag it in the direction you want to rotate the line. To change its size, press the object's resize handle (the white circle), and then drag it to increase or reduce the line's size. (Just like the Shapes tool!)

To delete a line from a page, select the line and choose **Delete** from the menu arrow. You can also press the Delete key on your keyboard or use the red X on the toolbar.

Hands-on Practice

Ready to give your new Notebook skills a try? Open the *Practicing SMART Skills.notebook* file and click on the arrow next to "Shapes and Lines Tools."

Watch the DVD

Want to learn more tips on working with Shapes and Lines Tools? Watch "Shapes and Lines Tools" on the DVD.

The Gallery

The Gallery contains clip art, pictures, backgrounds, multimedia content, Notebook files, and pages that you can use to jazz up your lessons. We will explore two of its main components—Gallery Essentials and the Lesson Activity Toolkit. But first, let's take a look at how the Gallery works.

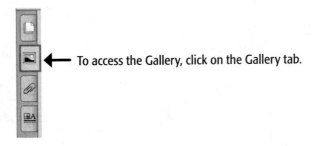

← To access the Gallery, click on the Gallery tab.

To search the Gallery, type a keyword into the *Type search terms here* box, and then press *Search* 🔍 . The Gallery will display all content containing the keyword.

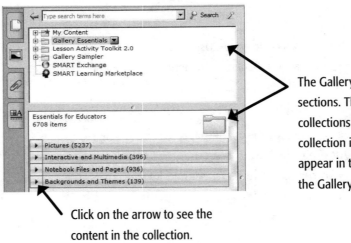

The Gallery is divided into two sections. The top section is the collections list. When you select a collection in the list, its contents appear in the bottom section of the Gallery.

Click on the arrow to see the content in the collection.

The bottom section of the gallery is divided into categories of objects. This makes it easy to find the object you are looking for. The number after each category indicates the number of objects in that category.

| ▶ Pictures (5237) |
| ▶ Interactive and Multimedia (396) |
| ▶ Notebook Files and Pages (936) |
| ▶ Backgrounds and Themes (139) |

Pictures – contains clipart and images.

Interactive and Multimedia – contains interactive objects such as videos, objects with sounds, or Adobe Flash elements. This is where the action is!

Notebook Files and Pages – contains designed pages that can be inserted into your file.

Backgrounds and Themes – contains a variety of styles that make your pages look visually appealing. Think of them like design templates in PowerPoint.

To add an object from the Gallery to a page, simply double-click on the object or drag the object to the page.

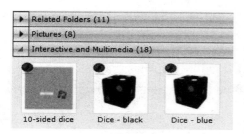

Double-click on an object in the Gallery to add it to the page. You can move the object to its desired location by dragging it. Change the object's size by selecting it and dragging the white circle to make the object larger or smaller. Rotate the object by dragging on the green circle.

Gallery Essentials

Gallery Essentials is a collection of thousands of images, multimedia content, and more, organized into subject-specific categories.

Click on the plus (+) sign to see the collections of content.

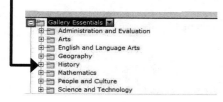

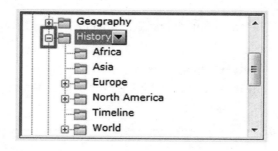

To locate the objects for that subject, look at the lower part of the Gallery.

Lesson Activity Toolkit

The Lesson Activity Toolkit is a collection of customizable tools and templates that you can use to create professional-looking and interactive lessons. The Toolkit helps you create engaging content like word games, quizzes, and sorting activities. It also offers Adobe Flash tools, such as hide-and-reveal and drag-and-drop.

Click on the plus (+) sign to see the categories of content.

Activities – contains a wide variety of interactive templates that can be customized to any subject. This is one of the best sections in the entire gallery! Don't miss out on it!

Examples – contains activities that contain content. Browse through them, edit them, and get ideas from them.

Games – contains images of board games, such as checkers and chess, cards, dominoes, and interactive crossword puzzles and number puzzles.

Graphics – contains icons, labels, tabs, buttons, and so on.

Pages – contains page templates to make your lessons look more professional.

Tools – contains a wide variety of interactive tools to make lessons more engaging and fun. This is another section you should not miss!

Watch the DVD

Want to learn more tips on how to utilize the Gallery? Watch "The Gallery" on the DVD.

Hands-on Practice

Ready to give your new Notebook skills a try? Open the *Practicing SMART Skills.notebook* file and click on the arrow next to "The Gallery."

Locking Down Objects

Oftentimes you will want to prevent certain objects from moving around on a Notebook page, especially in activities that call for students to come up and interact with objects on the board. It is simple to lock down objects in SMART Notebook software.

Below is a simple T-chart in which students can write nouns and verbs in the correct columns. You would not want them to accidentally move around the T-chart or the labels. To lock an object down, click on the object, then on its menu arrow. Select **Locking > Lock in Place**. Now the object cannot accidentally get moved.

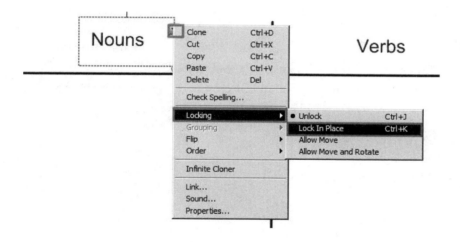

If you need to unlock the object, click on the object, click on the lock, and select **Unlock**.

Grouping and Layering Objects

As you begin to create lessons in SMART Notebook software, you will find many uses for grouping and layering objects. Let's take a look at how easy it is to do!

Layering

By default, whatever object you put on your page first is automatically at the back layer. The next object will be on the layer in front of it, the next one will be in front of that, and so on.

However, you may want to change the order of objects. To change the order, click on the object, then on its menu arrow. Select *Order*, and choose *Send Backward* or *Bring Forward*. To put an object in the bottom layer, choose *Send to Back*. To put it on the top layer, choose *Bring to Front*.

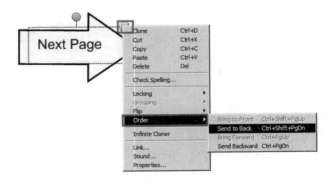

Watch the DVD

Want to learn more tips on how to use the grouping and layering features? Watch "Grouping and Layering Objects" on the DVD.

Grouping

When you add objects (text, lines, shapes, images, and so on) on the page, each item added on the SMART Board is a separate element. At times, you may want to group items so that an entire section of the page can be moved together. After you group the objects, you can select, move, rotate, resize, or flip the group as if it were an individual object.

To group objects together, click the Select icon . Click on the page and drag until a rectangle surrounds all the objects you want to select. A selection rectangle appears around the selected objects. Click the menu arrow of any one of the selected objects, and then select **Grouping > Group**.

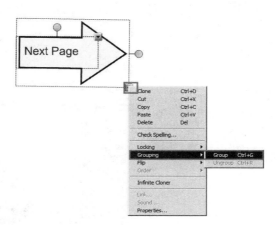

To ungroup objects, click the group's menu arrow, and then select **Grouping > Ungroup**.

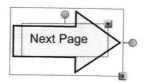

Hands-on Practice

Ready to give your new Notebook skills a try? Open the *Practicing SMART Skills.notebook* file and click on the arrow next to "Grouping and Layering."

Cloning

The cloning tool in SMART Notebook is very versatile. It allows you to create a duplicate of an object by using the Clone command, or create multiple copies of an object using the Infinite Cloner command.

Clone

Want to make an exact copy of an object? Simply select the object by clicking on it, click on the menu arrow, and choose *Clone*. An exact copy of the object is made. You can also use the keyboard command *Control+D*.

Put $1.25 in the cash register.

Infinite Cloner

When you want to make multiple copies of the same object, use the Infinite Cloner.

Select the object by clicking on it, click on the menu arrow, and choose *Infinite Cloner*.

Extend the pattern.

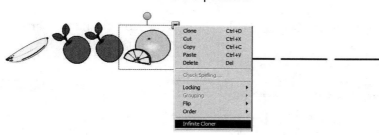

Once you have turned on the Infinite Cloner for an object, an infinity symbol (∞) will appear when you click on the object.

To utilize the Infinite Cloner, simply click and drag on the object and a copy will be made automatically. This can be repeated as many times as desired.

To turn off the Infinite Cloner, click on the object, then click on the infinity symbol. You can then deselect *Infinite Cloner*.

Tip:

When the Infinite Cloner tool is turned on, you will not be able to move or edit the object.

Hands-on Practice

Ready to give your new Notebook skills a try? Open the *Practicing SMART Skills.notebook* file and click on the arrow next to "Cloning Tools."

Screen Shade

If you want to cover information and reveal it slowly during a presentation, you can add a Screen Shade to a page. The Screen Shade is an easy yet incredible way to grab students' attention and add suspense to your lessons.

To turn on the Screen Shade, click on the icon on the toolbar.

↑
Screen Shade

The Screen Shade will cover the entire page. The small circles at the edges of the Screen Shade are resize handles. Press and drag the resize handle to reveal part of a page. To remove the entire Screen Shade, click on the red exit button on the upper right-hand corner or click on the Screen Shade icon again.

Guess My Number
I am a 3-digit number.

Close the
Screen Shade
by clicking
here.

Drag the Screen Shade using
one of the resize handles.

Tip:

The Screen Shade can be manipulated in four directions. You can pull it up or down, left or right.

Dual Page Display

Sometimes it is handy to display two pages at the same time. You can put two pages on view side-by-side with the Dual Page Display feature. There are many reasons to display two pages at a time. For example, you might show a graph or a reading passage on one page and have questions about it displayed on the other page.

To show two Notebook pages at the same time, click the Dual Page Display icon.

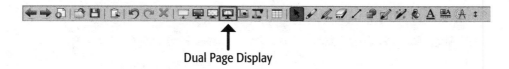

Dual Page Display

A second page appears in the whiteboard area.

What kind of pizza would you like?	
Cheese	10
Sausage	3
Pepperoni	12
Vegi	1
Supreme	8

Pizza Questions

What is the total number of votes received?

A red border indicates the active page.
Simply click on a page to make it active.

To return back to a single-page display, simply click on the Dual Page Display icon again.

Tip:

Objects can be easily moved from one page to another simply by dragging them.

Pin Page

When you're displaying dual Notebook pages, you can "pin" down one page so it stays in place in the whiteboard area while you scroll through other pages. This feature comes in handy when you have a series of questions that relate to one page.

First, you will need to add the Pin Page icon 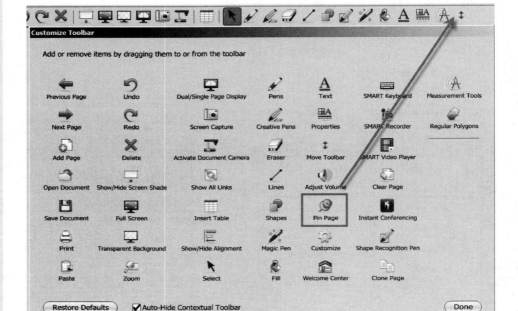 to your toolbar. Right-click on the SMART Notebook toolbar to open a window with additional tools for customizing your toolbar. Click and drag the Pin Page icon on to the toolbar, then click **Done**. Now the Pin Page icon will always be available on your toolbar.

Click the icon and drag it to the toolbar.

While in Dual Page Display mode, navigate to the page you would like to pin. Click on the page to make it the active page (look for the red border around the page). Then click on the Pin Page icon. You can now navigate through the other pages while the pinned page remains in place.

To unpin a page, click on the Pin Page icon again.

Tables

Tables can make your SMART Board lessons more exciting! After you create a table, you can insert objects into the table's cells, including freehand objects, geometric shapes, straight lines, text, and graphics files. You can also use a feature called a Cell Shade for even more dynamic lessons.

Inserting a Table

To insert a table on the page, click on the Table icon.

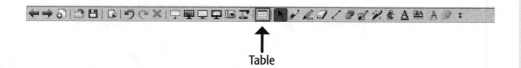

Table

A grid will appear below the toolbar. Move the pointer over the grid to select the number of columns and rows that you want in the table. The cells of the grid correspond to the cells of your table. The table will appear on the page.

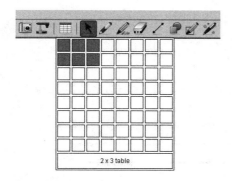

2 x 3 table

Moving a Table

To move the table, press the square in the table's upper left corner, and then drag the table to a different position on the page.

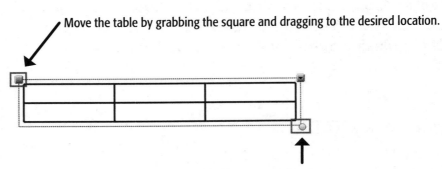

Move the table by grabbing the square and dragging to the desired location.

Make the entire table smaller or larger by dragging the resize handle (white circle).

OR

Select all the table's cells, and then drag the cells to a different place on the page.

Resizing Columns and Rows

To resize a column, drag a border to the desired width.

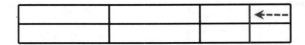

To resize a row, drag a border to the desired height.

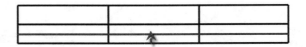

Adding Columns and Rows

To add a column to the table, select all the cells in one column. Right-click in the column, and select **Insert Column**. A new column appears to the right of the current column. To remove a column, follow the same steps, but select **Delete Column**.

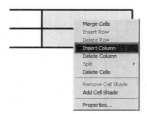

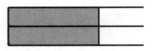

Tip:

Make sure you have the entire column selected before right-clicking.

To add a row to the table, select all the cells in one row. Right-click in the row, and select **Insert Row**. A new row appears below the current row. To remove a row, follow the same steps, but select **Delete Row**.

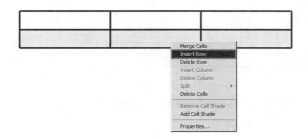

Adding Cell Color

You can add color to a cell, row, column, or an entire table. To change the properties of a table, column, row, cell, or multiple cells, select the desired cells and click on the Properties tab.

Select the desired fill effect—solid fill, gradient fill, pattern fill, or image fill.

Properties ➔ tab

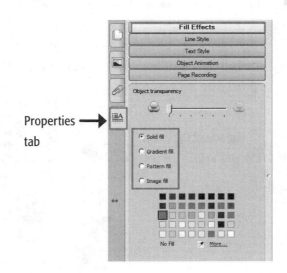

Adding Text to a Table

There are two ways you can add text to a cell. The first method is to type your text OUTSIDE of the table (any place on the page) and then drag the words into the desired cell. When you drag the text to the cell, the cell will automatically resize to fit the text.

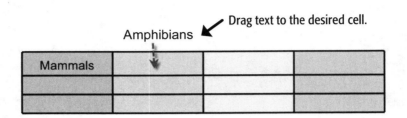

The second method is to double-click on a cell and type directly in the cell.

Notice the Font toolbox appears.

Double-click in a cell and start typing.

Adding Images or Other Objects to a Table

Any object can be added to a table cell. Images can be placed on the page or dragged straight from the Gallery into a cell. Images will resize to fit the cell.

Drag the animal to the correct column.

The size of the image changes to fit in the cell.

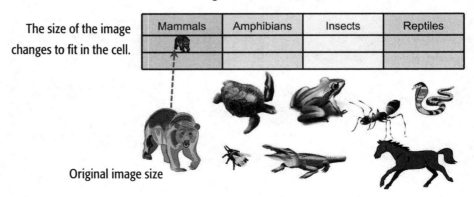

Original image size

Removing an Object From a Table

To remove an object from a table, select the object and drag it out of the cell.

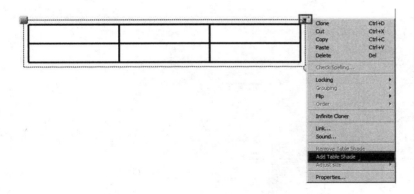

Mammals	Amphibians	Insects	Reptiles

Adding a Table Shade or Cell Shade

Cell shades are a fun and interactive way of using tables in your lessons. Using a cell shade enables you to reveal the information in the cells slowly during a presentation.

To add a shade to an entire table, select the table and click on the table's menu arrow. Select **Add Table Shade**.

Clone	Ctrl+D
Cut	Ctrl+X
Copy	Ctrl+C
Paste	Ctrl+V
Delete	Del
Check Spelling...	
Locking	▸
Grouping	▸
Flip	▸
Order	▸
Infinite Cloner	
Link...	
Sound...	
Remove Table Shade	
Add Table Shade	
Adjust size	▸
Properties...	

Pick a cell and solve the problem!

•	•	•
•	32*7+6	•

Once a table shade has been added, simply click on any cell to remove its shade. This action can be used to slowly reveal information placed in the table.

You can also add a cell shade to just one cell or multiple cells. Select the desired cell or cells, right-click, and click **Add Cell Shade**.

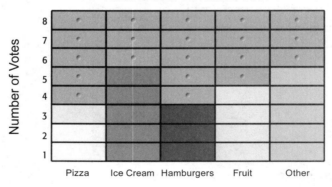

Question	Check Your Answer
What is the Kansas state flower?	Sunflower
What is the Kansas state tree?	
What is the Kansas state insect?	

Drag your cursor to select the cells you want, then right-click and select **Add Cell Shade**.

Creating a Bar Graph Activity

Use the table to create a simple bar graph activity. For example, say you ask students to vote for their favorite food. First, create the table. Then, add color to the columns. Finally, add a table shade. Call on each student to cast a vote by clicking on a cell above his or her favorite food.

What is Your Favorite Food?

Number of Votes

| 8 | 7 | 6 | 5 | 4 | 3 | 2 | 1 |

Pizza   Ice Cream   Hamburgers   Fruit   Other

Tip:

You must remove the Cell Shade if you want to change the table's properties; resize the table, a column, or a row; insert columns or rows; or remove columns, rows, or cells. It is best to do all the formatting of the table before adding the Cell Shades.

Watch the DVD

Want to learn more tips on how to utilize tables in your Notebook lessons? Watch "Tables" on the DVD.

Hands-on Practice

Ready to give your new Notebook skills a try? Open the *Practicing SMART Skills.notebook* file and click on the arrow next to "Tables."

Saving, Printing, Exporting

SMART Notebook software makes saving, printing, and exporting your Notebook lessons a breeze and allows for more flexibility in sharing your lessons with students.

Saving Your Files

Saving your SMART Notebook files is exactly the same as saving files in other applications. (It is very similar to the one in PowerPoint, which lets you save multiple slides or pages in a single file.)

For a brand-new file, click on the Save icon on the toolbar or click *File > Save as*.

The Save As dialog box appears. Browse to the folder where you want to save the new file. Type a name for the file in the *File name* box and click *Save*.

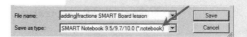

To save changes to an existing file, simply click the Save icon on the toolbar.

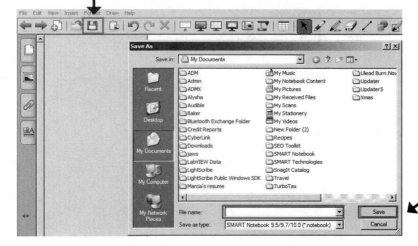

Decide where you would like to save your file. Give your file a name and click *Save*. All your pages will be saved into a single file.

If you want to save a file with a new name or location, click on *File > Save As*. Browse to the folder where you want to save the new file. Type a name for the file in the *File name* box and click *Save*.

Printing

SMART Notebook offers several options for printing your Notebook files. For example, you may want to print just one or two pages so students can have a copy of what you are showing on your SMART Board. To print files or pages, Select *File > Print*. The Print dialog box appears. You can select *Thumbnails*, *Handouts*, or *Full Page* in the *Print What* column.

Press the *Printer Setup* tab to select other print settings, including the printer name and the number of copies.

Decide if you want a header, footer, or the date to appear on your printed pages.

Choose between *Thumbnails*, *Handouts*, or *Full Page* printing.

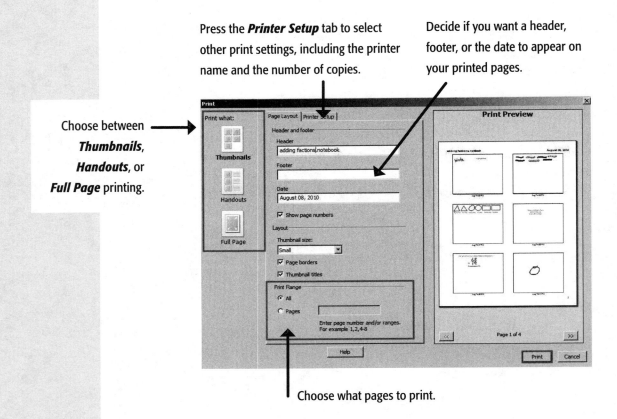

Choose what pages to print.

Exporting Files

You can export your file in a variety of formats, including HTML for a Web page, as images, or as a PDF. You can even export it into PowerPoint. One reason you may want to export your Notebook file to a different file type is so you can share your work with students or parents who do not have the SMART Notebook software on their computers.

To export a file, click on *File > Export*. Then choose your desired file format.

Tip:

When exporting a SMART Notebook file into another format, you will lose most of the interactivity of the SMART Notebook file. For example, you will not be able to drag and drop items into a table and Flash objects will not be active. Exporting is best when used to share lesson notes and basic information.

PART 2

Beyond the Basics

Now that you've learned the basics, it's time to move on to more exciting stuff! In addition to customizing Notebook's basic tools, you'll also learn how to create hyperlinks, animate objects, capture images from the screen, import and export files, and more. Let's get going!

Customizing Tools

Many of the tools in SMART Notebook can be customized to meet your specific needs and tastes. Do you prefer to have your default font blue and bold using Comic Sans? No problem! Want your pens to reflect your school's colors? No worries! In this section, you will learn how to customize fonts, pens, lines, and shapes tools.

Customizing Text

To change the default font, click on the Text icon on the toolbar. Select the "A" on the left of the text toolbar. Then click on the Properties tab.

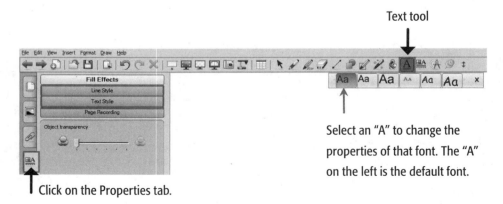

Text tool

Select an "A" to change the properties of that font. The "A" on the left is the default font.

Click on the Properties tab.

Click on *Line Style* and select the color you would like for the font.

Then click on *Text Style* and choose the font, size, and style you want.

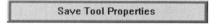

To save your choices, click *Save Tool Properties*.

Tip:

When you are finished changing the font, be sure to go back to the toolbar and click on the Select tool.

Customizing Pens

To customize the pens, click on the Pens icon on the toolbar, and then click on the pen you would like to change.

Pens tool

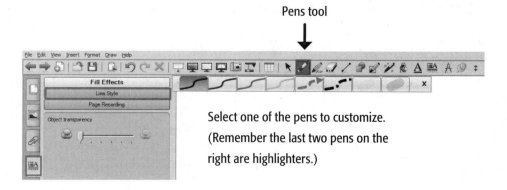

Select one of the pens to customize. (Remember the last two pens on the right are highlighters.)

Click on the Properties tab.

Tip:

The pens in the pen tray can be customized as well. Open the Welcome Center and then click on **Control Panel**. Choose **SMART Hardware Settings** and find **Pen Tray Settings**. Make your desired choices. (You must be hooked up to a SMART Board in order to make changes to the settings.)

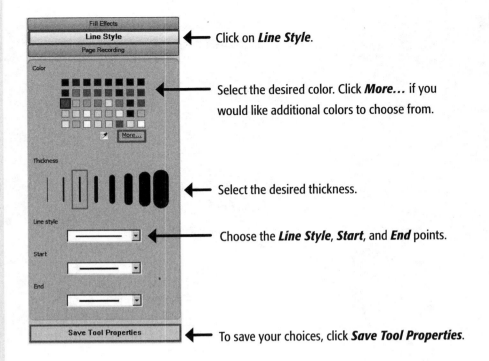

Click on **Line Style**.

Select the desired color. Click **More...** if you would like additional colors to choose from.

Select the desired thickness.

Choose the **Line Style**, **Start**, and **End** points.

To save your choices, click **Save Tool Properties**.

Customizing Lines

Customizing lines is almost identical to customizing pens. Click the Lines icon on the toolbar, and then click on the line you would like to change.

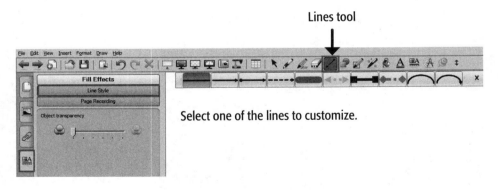

Lines tool

Select one of the lines to customize.

Click on the Properties tab.

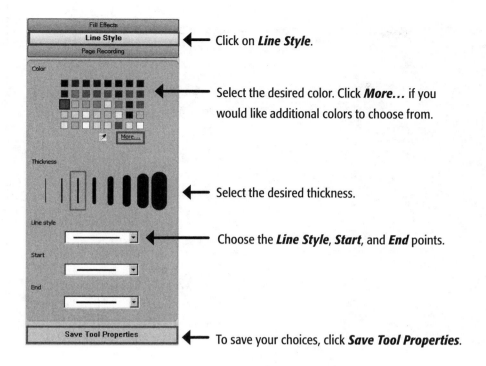

← Click on *Line Style*.

← Select the desired color. Click *More...* if you would like additional colors to choose from.

← Select the desired thickness.

← Choose the *Line Style*, *Start*, and *End* points.

← To save your choices, click *Save Tool Properties*.

Customizing Shapes

To customize a shape, click on the Shapes icon on the toolbar, and then click on the shape you would like to change.

Shapes tool

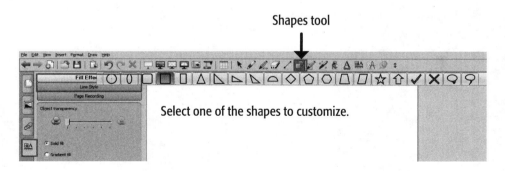

Select one of the shapes to customize.

Click on the Properties tab.

When you customize a shape, you have a few more options available than when you customize a line or pen. You can choose the line style (outline) as well as the fill effects. Get creative by filling the image with a gradient color or even an image.

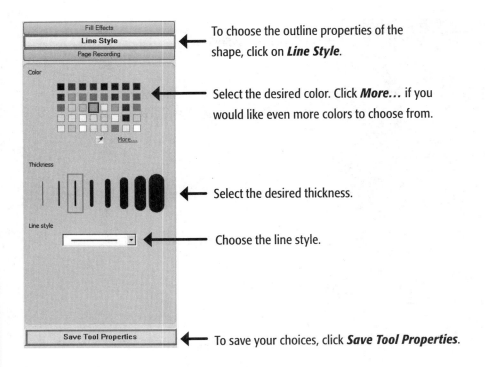

To choose the outline properties of the shape, click on **Line Style**.

Select the desired color. Click **More...** if you would like even more colors to choose from.

Select the desired thickness.

Choose the line style.

To save your choices, click **Save Tool Properties**.

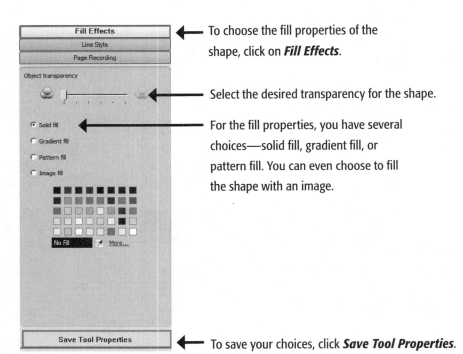

To choose the fill properties of the shape, click on **Fill Effects**.

Select the desired transparency for the shape.

For the fill properties, you have several choices—solid fill, gradient fill, or pattern fill. You can even choose to fill the shape with an image.

To save your choices, click **Save Tool Properties**.

Watch the DVD

Want to learn more tips on how to customize the tools in SMART Notebook? Watch "Customizing Tools" on the DVD.

Hands-on Practice

Ready to give your new Notebook skills a try? Open the *Practicing SMART Skills.notebook* file and click on the arrow next to "Customizing Tools."

Hyperlinks

Hyperlinks are links that can be clicked on to take you to a Web site, to another page in the file, or to another document. Hyperlinks can be used in a variety of ways in lessons and can increase student engagement and the interactivity of your lesson.

Making a Hyperlink to a Web site

Creating a hyperlink to a Web site is a breeze. Go to the Internet and browse to the Web site you would like to create a link to. Copy its URL.

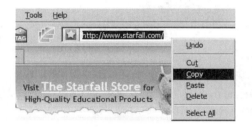

To copy a URL, highlight it, and then right-click and choose *Copy*. Another way to copy is to highlight the URL and click *Control+C* on your keyboard.

Go to the page in SMART Notebook where you want the hyperlink and paste the link.

Right-click on the page and select *Paste*. Alternatively, you can click *Control+V* on your keyboard.

http://www.starfall.com/

The URL is pasted on to the SMART Notebook page and can be easily accessed by clicking on the small globe icon in the lower-left corner.

You can also attach a hyperlink to a piece of text or to an object. This method produces a more visually appealing link.

In this example, we will attach a Web site's URL to text. First, type the desired text. Next, click the menu arrow on the text box, and then click **Link...**.

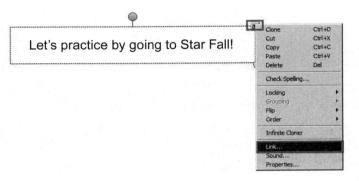

Choose **Web Page** on the left and then type or paste the URL in the box. Click **OK**.

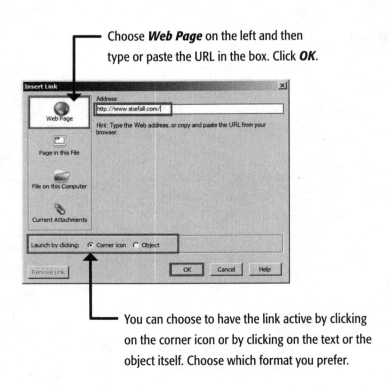

You can choose to have the link active by clicking on the corner icon or by clicking on the text or the object itself. Choose which format you prefer.

Let's practice by going to Star Fall! ⬅   **This is what the link looks like now.**

To attach a hyperlink to a shape or object, follow the same steps as above.

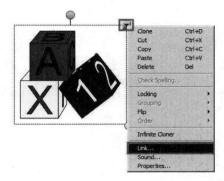

Click on the menu arrow and select *Link*....

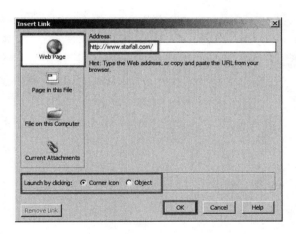

Paste the URL and decide how you want the link to be launched. Click *OK*.

This is what the link looks now – pretty nice, isn't it?

Making a Hyperlink to Another Page in the File

Creating a hyperlink to another page in your SMART Notebook file is very similar to making a link to a Web page. You can attach the link to text or an object. Before you create a link, make sure you have already created the page you plan to link to.

Evaluate 3 + 6x (5 + 4) + 3 − 7 using the order of operations.

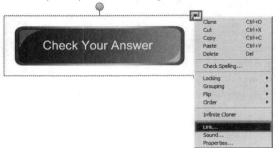

Click on the menu arrow of the object or text and click **_Link…._**

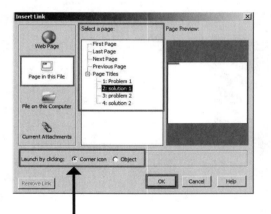

On the left side of the window, choose **_Page in this File_**. The pages in your file will appear on the right side. Choose the desired page.

Decide if you want to launch the link by clicking on the corner icon or on the object itself, then click **_OK_**.

Linking to another page in the file is a great way to create self-checking pages for students. For example, say you create a multiple-choice quiz on a page. You can set up the choices so that when students click on the correct answer, it links them to a feedback page that displays "Great Job!" Alternatively, if they click on a wrong answer, it could take them to a page that says "Try Again."

Linking to a File on Your Computer

Sometimes you might want to link a document directly to your SMART Notebook lesson. The process for attaching a file is very similar to that of creating a hyperlink to a Web site. Documents can be attached to text or an object.

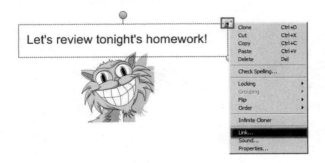

Click on the menu arrow of the object or text and click *Link...*.

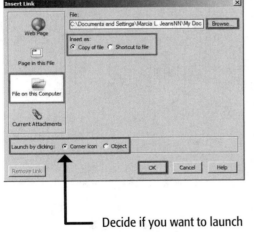

Click on *File on this Computer*.

Click on *Browse* and locate the file on your computer. Decide if you want a copy of the file to be attached or just a shortcut to the file. If you plan to transfer your lesson to another computer, choose *Copy of file*. This will ensure a copy of the file gets transferred along with your Notebook lesson.

Decide if you want to launch the file by clicking on the corner icon or on the object itself, then click *OK*.

Hands-on Practice

Ready to give your new Notebook skills a try? Open the *Practicing SMART Skills.notebook* file and click on the arrow next to "Hyperlinks."

Animation

Adding animations to a lesson is yet another way to make exciting activities that will enhance the content you are teaching. If you are familiar with adding animations in PowerPoint then you will have no problem creating animations in SMART Notebook!

Tip:

One fun way to use animation in a lesson is to put a text or picture under an animated object. When students touch the object, the text or picture is revealed! In the example below, the ovals have been set to fade out when clicked on, revealing a famous person.

You can animate any object or text to fly onto a page, spin, fade in, shrink, and more. You can also set the animation to start when you open a page or when you click on the object. Follow these steps to animate an object.

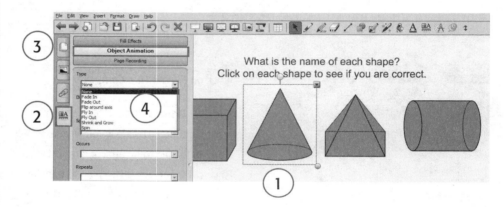

1. Click on the object you would like to animate.

2. Click on the Properties tab.

3. Click on **Object Animation**.

4. Click on the type of animation you would like (e.g., fade in or out, flip around axis, spin, and so on).

After selecting the type of animation, you can choose the direction, speed, occurrence, and number of repeats, depending on the type of animation.

Hands-on Practice

Ready to give your new Notebook skills a try? Open the *Practicing SMART Skills.notebook* file and click on the arrow next to "Animation."

Screen Capture Tools

The Screen Capture tools allow you to easily capture images from the Internet, remove unwanted portions of an image, and take a screenshot of your computer screen. You will find these tools to be quite handy!

There are four types of screen captures you can perform:

Window Capture – selects the window that you want to appear in the screen capture

Full Screen Capture – captures the entire screen

Area Capture – selects an area you want to capture. Click this button, and then drag your mouse to select the area.

Freehand Capture – allows you to define the area you want to capture. Simply click and drag the crosshairs on the screen.

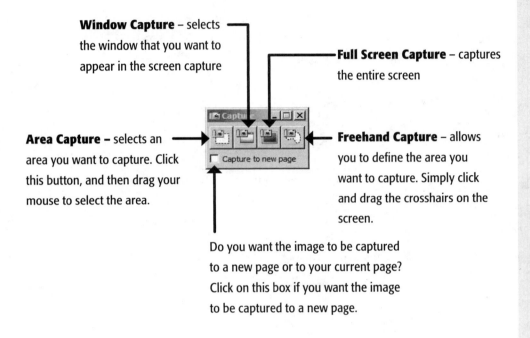

Do you want the image to be captured to a new page or to your current page? Click on this box if you want the image to be captured to a new page.

To Capture an Image From the Internet

In SMART Notebook, click on the Screen Capture icon.

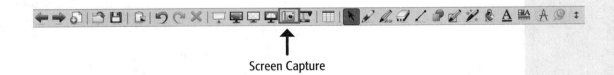

Screen Capture

The Screen Capture floating toolbar will appear. Go to the Web page where the image you want is located. Click on the left choice, the Area Capture, on the Screen Capture toolbar. If you want the image to appear on the current page, make sure the **Capture to new page** choice is unchecked.

The pointer changes to crosshairs. Press and drag the crosshairs on the screen to define the area you want to capture.

An image of the area will appear on your SMART Notebook page. You can then drag it to the desired location on the page. In this example, you can now add hyperlinks that would take you directly to certain Web sites.

Removing Unwanted Portions of an Image

Using the Screen Capture tool, you can remove unwanted portions of an image. For example, say you want to remove half of this butterfly image to create a lesson on symmetry.

Can you draw the other half of the butterfly to show its symmetry?

Click on the Screen Capture icon.

The Screen Capture floating toolbar will appear. Click on the left choice, the Area Capture, on the Screen Capture toolbar.

Press and drag the crosshairs on the screen to define the area you want to capture; in this case, the half of the butterfly you want to keep.

Can you draw the other half of the butterfly to show its symmetry?

The copied section of the image will appear on the page.

Can you draw the other half of the butterfly to show its symmetry?

Simply delete the original image from the page and drag the copied image to the desired location.

Take a Screenshot of Your Computer Screen

Using the Screen Capture tool, you can take a screenshot of your computer screen, whether you are using a software application or browsing the Internet, or just want a screenshot of your desktop.

Click on the Screen Capture icon. The Screen Capture floating toolbar will appear. Go to the computer screen you would like to capture.

Depending on your preferences, choose either Window Capture or Full Screen Capture on the toolbar. The captured image will appear on your page.

Here is an example of a window capture.

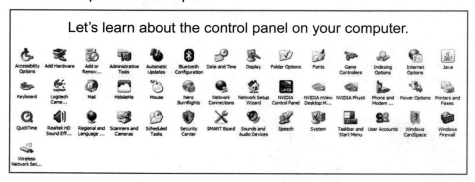

Here is an example of a screen capture.

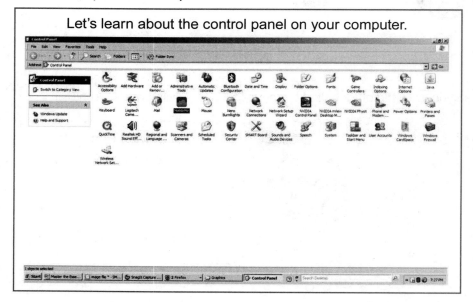

Adding Graphics

The SMART Notebook Gallery contains thousands of images, but it may not always have exactly what you are looking for. You can insert images into your Notebook file from the Internet or from files saved on your computer.

Inserting a Picture From the Internet

Go to the Web page where the image you want is located.

Right-click on the image and choose **Copy Image** (or **Copy As...**, depending on the browser you are using).

Navigate to the SMART Notebook page where you would like to insert the image.

Right-click on the page and choose **Paste**. The image will appear on your page and can be resized or moved to another place on the page.

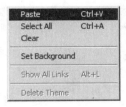

Keep copyright laws in mind when using images from the Internet. A great source for copyright-friendly images is **Pics4Learning**: http://www.pics4learning.com. This Web site grants teachers and students permission to use any of its thousands of images, donated by students, teachers, and amateur photographers.

Tip:

When resizing an image, hold down the Shift key as you drag the resize handle. This ensures the image will retain its proportions.

Inserting an Image Saved on Your Computer

If you have an image on your computer that you'd like to insert into your Notebook page, click on **Insert > Picture File**.

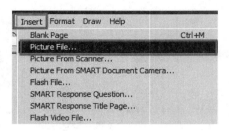

Browse to where the picture is located on your computer. Select the desired picture by clicking on it, and then click **Open**. The picture will appear on your Notebook page and can be resized or moved to another place on the page.

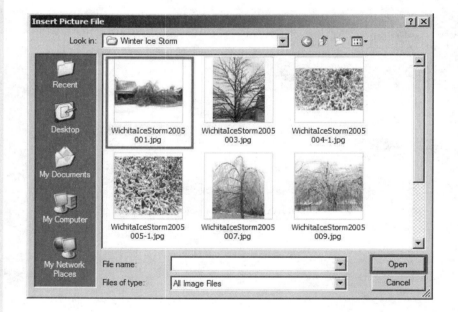

Tip:

There are several interactive objects in the Lesson Activity Toolkit section of the Gallery that work perfectly with images. Simply click on *Lesson Activity Toolkit* at the top section of the Gallery, then click on *Interactive and Multimedia* at the bottom section.

Here are a few interactive objects you may want to explore:

Object Name	How to Use	Sample
Dice – Image	Customize this six-sided, interactive die by inserting a picture on each of its faces.	
Question Flipper – Image	Insert an image on one side of the flipper and another image or text on the other side. When you touch the flipper, it flips to the other side.	
Random Image Selector	Insert up to 36 images, and the tool will randomly pick one of them. Great to use as a random student selector.	
Image Match	Insert up to five images for students to match with their labels.	

Here's another easy way to find image tools in the Gallery.

Click on the Gallery tab.

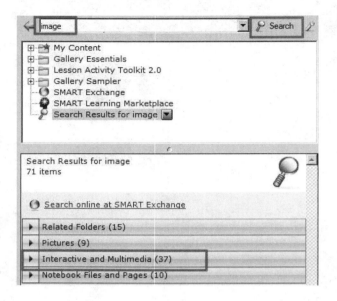

Type "image" in the search box and click **Search**.

Browse the *Interactive and Multimedia* section.

My Content

My Content is a Gallery tool that allows you to save and organize your own collection of images, objects, and pages so you can easily access and reuse them in the future. You can also export this collection and send it to others to install in their own galleries.

Before you start adding objects to My Content, you may want to think first about how you want to organize them. For example, you may want to organize them by subject area. You can create folders and subfolders for each subject to help you easily find objects in the future.

Click on the Gallery tab.

Select *My Content* in the Gallery's category list. Click its menu arrow and then select *New Folder*.

A new folder appears. By default, the new folder's name is "Untitled." Type a new name for the subcategory.

Create as many folders and subfolders as desired.

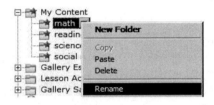

To rename a folder, select the folder and then click its menu arrow. Click on **Rename** and give the folder a new name.

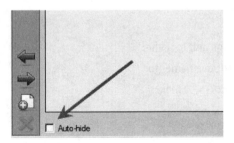

To add an object to My Content, make sure the **Auto-hide** checkbox at the bottom of the screen is unchecked.

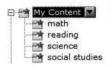

Objects can be dragged from a Notebook page into the desired folder.

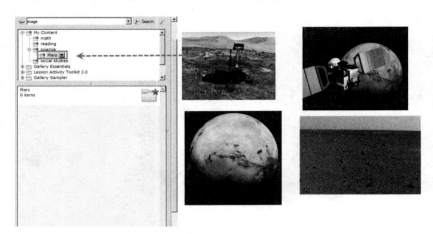

Once you have inserted the object into the desired folder, you can give the object a name.

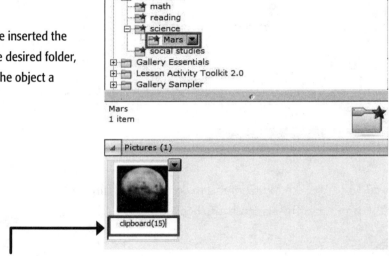

Double-click on the name of the image and type the new name. Giving the object a descriptive name (for example, "Mars" instead of "clipboard(15)") makes searching for it easier.

Almost any type of object can be added to My Content. In addition to images, you can add the following:

Text – Type students' names on a Notebook page, each one in its own text box. Drag each text box to a folder and rename each object with the student's name. Anytime you want to use students' names in an activity, you won't have to retype them.

Graphic organizers – Use the Shapes tool to create a graphic organizer, group it, and save it to My Content. Whenever you want to use the graphic organizer, simply click and drag it out on the page.

Templates – Create a template for routines that occur every day, like the daily agenda. Once you have created the template, add the entire page to the Gallery. Simply click on the menu arrow of the thumbnail, and choose *Add Page to Gallery*.

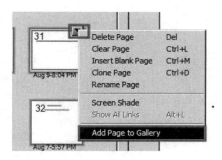

Export and Share My Content

Sharing a folder from My Content with other teachers is easy to do!

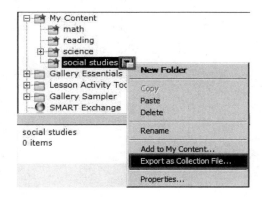

Click on the menu arrow of the folder you would like to export (or export your entire My Content folder.) Choose *Export as Collection File....*

Give the collection a name, then decide where to save it on your computer. Click **Save**.

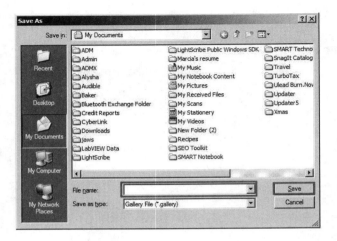

A Gallery Collection file is created. This file can be e-mailed (as long as the file size isn't too large), saved on a jump drive, or placed on a shared server.

social
studies.gallery

To install a Gallery Collection, simply save the file on a computer and double-click on it. SMART Notebook will open and the collection will automatically be installed in My Content.

Importing Files

You can import a variety of file types, such as PowerPoint, PDFs, and Word documents, into SMART Notebook. Importing such files gives you access to the features and functions of SMART Notebook that you would not otherwise have in the original file.

Importing a PowerPoint Presentation

To import a PowerPoint presentation into SMART Notebook, click on *File > Import*.

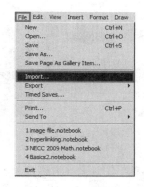

Browse to the location of the PowerPoint file, select it, and click **Open**.

The PowerPoint file will be imported into SMART Notebook.
NOTE: PowerPoint animations do not transfer into SMART Notebook.

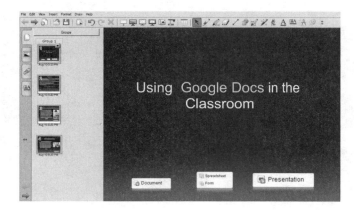

Importing PDFs

Teachers often have an abundance of curriculum materials in PDF format. You can easily take any of these materials and import it into SMART Notebook.

Open the PDF and click on *File > Print*.

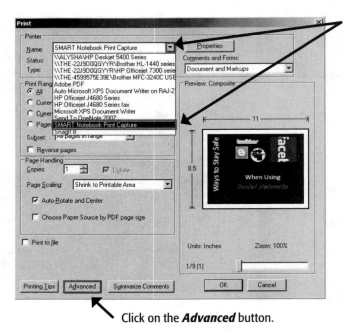

Click on the dropdown arrow for the printer name and select *SMART Notebook Print Capture*.

Click on the *Advanced* button.

Click on the *Print as image* box and click *OK*. Choosing this option will give the file a much cleaner look when you import it to SMART Notebook.

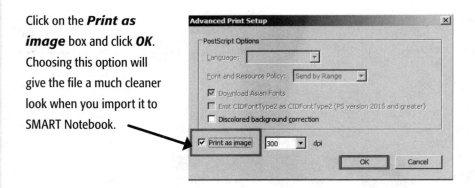

Decide what pages you would like to import into SMART Notebook by making your choice in the **_Print Range_** section. (Each page of the PDF will import as a new page in SMART Notebook.)

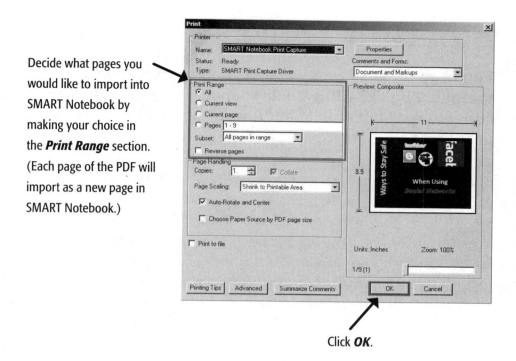

Click **_OK_**.

You will see a progress bar appear. If you have a large file, please be patient. It could take several minutes for the import to finish.

If you already have a Notebook file open, the PDF pages will be imported into it. If you do not have a Notebook file open, a new file will be created and opened when the import is complete.

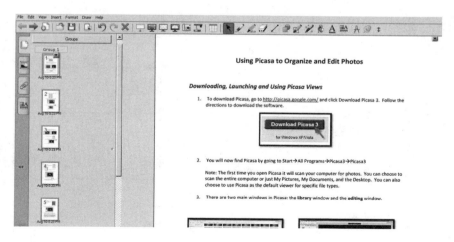

Floating Tools Toolbar

You may already be aware of the Floating Tools toolbar. The Floating Tools toolbar is a customizable collection of buttons that "floats" on top of other programs.

By default, the Floating Tools toolbar displays on your desktop and enables you to quickly access frequently used tools and features of SMART Notebook even when you are not using the software. For example, you can visit a Web site and highlight key features from the site using the highlighter from the Floating Tools or you can use the tools on other applications such as Microsoft Word or PowerPoint. The Floating Tools can be utilized with almost any application.

In its default mode, the Floating Tools toolbar contains the following:

Tool Name	Action
Select	Left-click
Pen	Write or draw in digital ink
Highlighter	Highlight in digital ink
Eraser	Erase digital ink
Right-Click	Right-click
Notebook	Create or open a *.notebook* file
Keyboard	Start SMART keyboard
Undo	Reverse the effect of your previous action
Customize	Customize the tools on the floating toolbar

You can customize the Floating Tools toolbar by clicking on the customize icon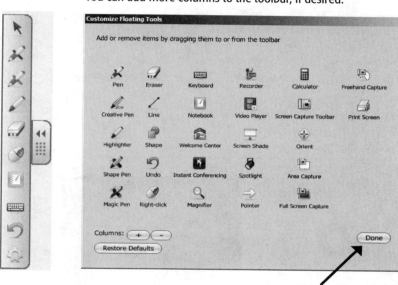

A variety of tools will appear that can be added to the toolbar. Add or remove items by dragging them to or from the toolbar.

You can add more columns to the toolbar, if desired.

Click **Done** to save your changes.

Removing the Floating Tools Toolbar

Sometimes you may not want the Floating Tools to show. To remove the toolbar, click on the SMART Board icon in the system tray.

SMART Board

Click on ***Hide Floating Tools***.

If you want the Floating Tools to reappear, simply repeat the process, and click on **Show Floating Tools**.

Instructional Ideas for the Floating Tools

1

Use the **Magnifier** to make a URL easier for students to read in the computer lab.

Magnifies by following the pointer on the screen.

Displays a red border around the magnified area. Try this option first.

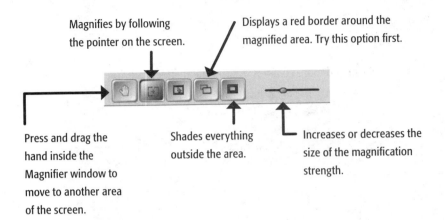

Press and drag the hand inside the Magnifier window to move to another area of the screen.

Shades everything outside the area.

Increases or decreases the size of the magnification strength.

2

Use the **Spotlight** tool to focus on a particular area.

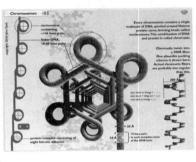 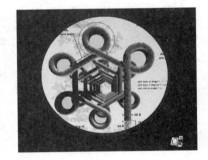

Some Web sites can have lots of distractions on the page. Use the Spotlight to focus students' attention to a specific area of the page.

3

Pen   Pointer

Use the **Pen** and **Pointer** in conjunction with other applications.

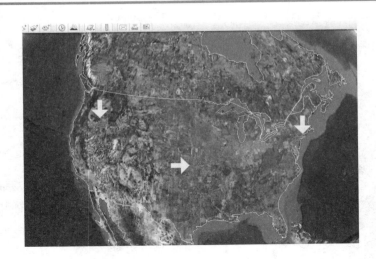

In the example above, the Pen and Pointer are used to help students better understand geography while using Google Earth.

Ink Aware

There may be times when you want to interact with a Microsoft Word, Excel, or PowerPoint file while using your SMART Board. Ink Aware is a feature that allows you to draw or write directly into these types of files and save your writing directly in the file.

Write or Draw in Microsoft Word or Excel

Open a Microsoft Word document or Excel spreadsheet. Pick up a pen from the SMART Board pen tray or from the Floating Tools toolbar and write on the document. The Ink Aware Tools toolbar will appear. Depending on your version of software, this toolbar either floats on top of the program or appears with the program's other toolbars.

Tip:

If the Aware Tools toolbar doesn't appear, pick up a pen from the pen tray or select a pen on the Floating Tools toolbar.

Press ![icon] to insert your notes or drawings into the file as graphics.

Press ![icon] to convert your writing into typed text and insert it into the file.

Press ![icon] to take a screen capture of your notes and the file. (The screen capture will appear in a SMART Notebook file.)

If desired, you can click on **Settings** on the Aware toolbar and have your drawings automatically inserted into the document as an image.

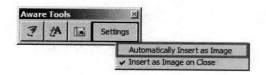

69

To Present a PowerPoint Presentation on a SMART Board

Open the PowerPoint file and display it in *Slide Show* view.

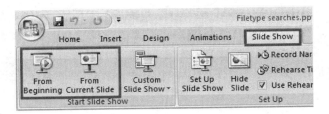

The PowerPoint slide show and the Slide Show toolbar will appear on your slide.

To go to the next slide, press Next on the Slide Show toolbar.

To go back the previous slide, press Previous on the Slide Show toolbar.

You can write or draw on the PowerPoint file and embed your notes into the presentation.

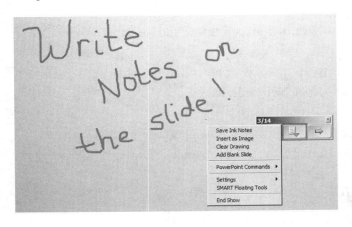

To insert notes or a drawing into the PowerPoint slide show as an image, press Menu on the Slide Show toolbar, and then select *Insert as Image*.

To clear notes on the current slide, press Menu , and then select *Clear Drawing*.

To restore your most recently deleted notes, press Menu , and then select *Restore Drawing*.

PART 3

Create Your Own Lessons

In this section, you'll find step-by-step instructions for creating a few activities using the various tools and features you've mastered from the previous sections. Enjoy!

MATH:

Find the Area

SMART TOOLS:

- Shapes tool
- Cloner
- Lines tool
- Text tool
- Pens tool
- Eraser

(1) Open a new Notebook page. In the Shapes tool, select the square shape. Click on the Notebook page and drag the cursor to create the square. Click on the square, then click on the Property tab. For **Line Style**, choose the thinnest line thickness and the pale purple color (next to white). For **Fill Effects**, choose **Solid fill** and a dark color, like blue. Move the square near the upper left-hand corner of the screen. Finally, click on the square's menu arrow and choose **Infinite Cloner**.

(2) Use the square to help you create a shape for students to measure. Drag from the infinitely cloned square until you have seven identical squares. Carefully position the squares to create the shape below. Make sure the squares merely touch each other and do not overlap.

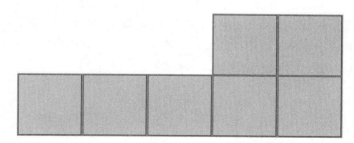

3 Select a solid line from the Lines tool and pick the thinnest line thickness. Choose a dark color or leave the line black. Using the squares as a guide, drag the cursor to create lines around and between the squares. When you have finished, click on each square and delete it. You'll be left with just a grid outline of the shape.

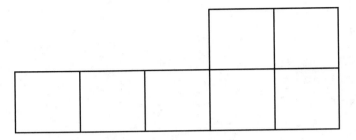

4 Using the Select tool, drag across the shape so that all the lines are selected. Click on one of the menu arrows and select *Grouping*, then *Group*. All the lines will now be grouped together. Move the shape to a desired spot. Then click on its menu arrow, select *Locking*, then *Lock in place*.

5 Click on a spot below the shape and type, "What is the area in square units?" Make sure the text is large enough to see on the board (font size should be at least 24 points). Lock the text box in place.

6 Click on the Shapes tool and select the rectangle shape. Click and drag to make a rectangle under the question, big enough to hold the answer. If you want, click on the rectangle and on the Properties tab to change its line style and color. Leave the inside of the rectangle white.

7 Click inside the rectangle and type the number "7." Select the number and make it boldfaced. Make the number as large as you can inside the box, then place it in the center.

8 Next, click on the Pens tool and then on the Properties tab. Select the thickest line thickness and the color white. Drag the pen over the number to hide it from view. Then click on the Select icon. (NOTE: Do not lock the white pen mark or it won't erase.)

9 Using a small font under the box, type "To check your answer, erase inside the box." Center the text box under the rectangle, then lock it in place.

10 Your math activity is ready to use! You can clone the page to create multiple copies, changing only the grid shape and the answer inside the box for each new page.

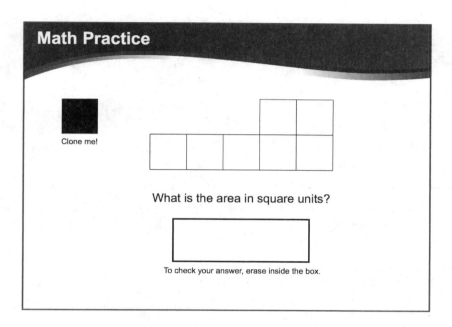

Math Practice

Clone me!

What is the area in square units?

To check your answer, erase inside the box.

Spin a Plural

1 Open a new Notebook page. Click on the Gallery tab and search for "spinner." In the bottom part of the Gallery, click the arrow for **Interactive and Multimedia**, then drag the spinner to the upper left corner of the page.

2 Click on the double arrow of the spinner to open a window where you can customize the spinner. For **Segments**, choose 3. Choose a large font size, like 34, and click **Apply all**. Next, click on one segment and in the **Text** box, type *-s*. Click on another segment and type *-es*. For the last segment, type *-ies*. You can also change the colors of the different segments if you want.

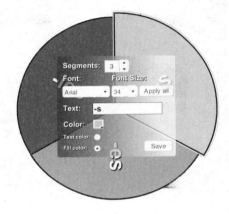

3 Next, click on the Shapes tool and select the star shape. While holding down the Shift key, drag the cursor until you have a star big enough for a word to fit inside. Change back to the Select tool and select the star you made. Click on the Properties tab to fill the star with a yellow color and give it a dark blue outline. Finally, click on the star's menu arrow to clone it so you have 12 identical stars.

4 Type the following words in separate text boxes: *banana, beach, candy, city, fox, hobby, house, puppy, sketch, sky, stamp, watch.* Make sure the words are big enough to fit inside the stars. (We used the Arial font, size 20.) Move each word inside a star and center it. The word should be in front of the star, as shown. If it's moving behind the star, click on the text's menu arrow and select **Order > Bring to Front**.

5 Using the Select tool, select a star and the word inside it to group them together. Click on a menu arrow, select **Grouping > Group**. Repeat for each of the other stars. When you have finished, move the stars to spread them around the page.

6 For each star, type the plural form of its word, using the same font and size. You might want to give the plural ending a different color to

highlight it. Place the word on the star to make sure it fits inside, then click on the text's menu arrow and select *Order > Send to Back*. The plural form should now be hidden behind each star.

7 Next, select a star, click on its menu arrow, and click on *Properties*. On the side window, select *Object Animation*. For *Type*, select *Fade out*, then select *When the object is clicked* for *Occur*. Click on the star's menu arrow again and select *Locking > Lock in Place*. Repeat for the rest of the stars.

8 Create an instruction box that can be tucked to one side. Start by typing these instructions: "Click on the spinner to get a plural ending. Find a word that you think uses that ending. Then click on the star to see if you're correct." Next, click on the Shapes tool and select the rectangle. Drag the cursor to create a box around the directions. (If you wish, you can go to the rectangle's *Properties* to select a line color and fill effect. Make sure to bring the text to front.) Click on the Shapes tool again and select the semicircle. Drag the cursor to make the semicircle about the same size as the rectangle's height. Click on the semicircle's green circle to rotate it on its side, then bring the semicircle next to rectangle. If necessary, drag on the white circle to adjust the semicircle's size to match the rectangle. Next, type the word "PULL" and make it boldfaced. Click on the text box's green circle, rotate it to its side, and move it inside the semicircle. Next, select all the different elements that make up the instruction box and group them together. Finally, tuck the instructions to one side of the page so that only the PULL tab is visible.

> **PULL** Click on the spinner to get a plural ending.
> Find a word that you think uses that ending.
> Then click on the star to see if you're correct.

9 Your language arts activity is ready to use! You can use the same template for math facts, state capitals, vocabulary words, and more.

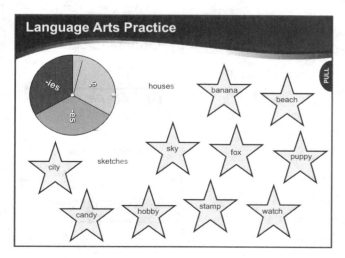

Language Arts Practice

SCIENCE:
Name That Animal!

1 Open a new Notebook page. Click on the Gallery tab and search for "butterfly." In the bottom part of the Gallery, click on the arrow for *Pictures* and choose the picture of a monarch butterfly. Drag it to the upper left corner of the page.

2 Under the butterfly, type the following prompts in one text box, leaving about two spaces between each line. Use a large font (Arial, size 24 or 26, boldface).

Common name:
Scientific name:
Aquatic or terrestrial:
Family and/or class:

Select the text box and click on its menu arrow. Select *Locking > Lock in Place*.

3 In separate text boxes, type the following:
Monarch butterfly
Danaus plexippus
Terrestrial
Nymphalidae

Center each word or phrase in its own text box. Then place each text box across from its corresponding label to create a second column. Using the Select tool, select all the text boxes. Then click on a menu arrow and select *Order > Bring to Front*.

4 Click on the Shapes tool and select the rectangle shape. Drag the cursor to create a rectangle around "Monarch butterfly" so that it's wide enough to cover the longest words in the list and deep enough so that it stops right on top of the next phrase, "*Danaus plexippus*," as shown. Click on the rectangle's menu arrow and select *Properties*. For both *Fill Effects* and *Line Style*, choose a dark blue or purple color. Then move the rectangle above the words in the second column.

Monarch butterfly
Danaus plexippus
Terrestrial
Nymphalidae

(5) Using the Select tool, select all four text boxes in the second column. Click on a menu arrow and select *Properties*. In the side window, select *Line Style* and choose the white color. All of the words should disappear into the background. Click on a menu arrow again and select *Locking > Lock in Place*.

(6) Click on the rectangle again and select *Properties*, then go to *Object Animation*. For *Type*, select *Flip around axis*. Under *Direction*, select *Bottom edge*, and for *Occurs*, select *When the object is clicked*. Click on the rectangle to test it. Each time you click, the rectangle will flip over along its bottom edge, revealing each of the white words in turn. You may have to adjust the position of the rectangle so that each word is centered in the box as it is revealed.

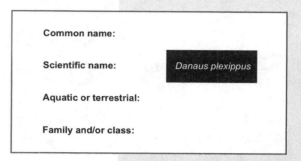

(7) Drag the rectangle back above the second column. Consider writing directions on the box so students know what to do. Type, "Click on the box to learn more about this animal." Make the text white and the font small enough to fit inside the box.

(8) Your science activity is ready to use! You can clone the page to create multiple copies, changing only the picture and the words in the second column for each new page.

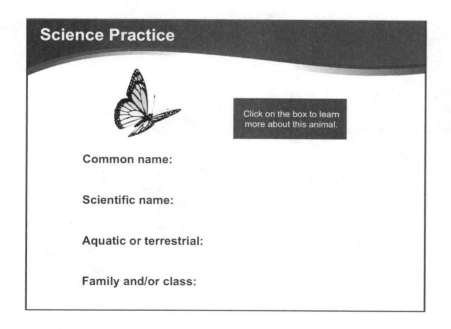

Professional Resources

Connect With Other Educators

One of the best ways to learn how to utilize your SMART Board is to connect to other teachers who are effectively using interactive whiteboard technology in their classrooms. The SMART Exchange, sponsored by SMART Technologies, is a free resource center and community network that provides a wealth of resources. You can exchange ideas and find the information you are looking for, including recent research, best practices, success stories, and daily tools. Collaborate with educators from around the globe and connect with a variety of SMART experts including product managers, content specialists, and technical support staff. You can even download lessons created by teachers or share a lesson you created with others!

SMART Exchange

http://exchange.smarttech.com

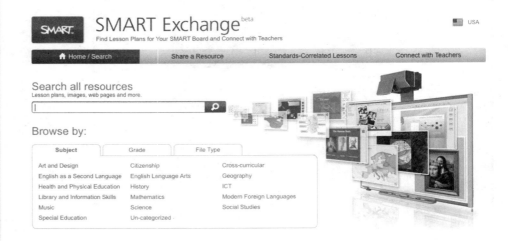

Top Web Sites for SMART Board Users

One of the greatest benefits to using a SMART Board is that there are thousands of other teachers just like you across the globe. And they like to share their tips and tricks, lessons, and other resources for using the SMART Board—on the Internet! Here are just a few of the top sites you should explore.

SMART's YouTube Channel

http://www.youtube.com/user/SMARTClassrooms

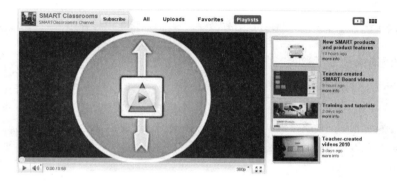

See SMART products in action around the world. Watch a wide variety of tutorials, get a leg up on new SMART products, and enjoy watching SMART Boards in action with your fellow teachers.

SMART Board Revolution

http://smartboardrevolution.ning.com

Share ideas, tips, and lesson files and collaborate to maximize students' learning on this social network geared for educators utilizing SMART Boards in the classroom.

Teachers Love SMART Boards

http://smartboards.typepad.com

 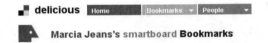

Jim Hollis has put together one of the most useful blogs around for SMART Board users. You'll certainly want to add his site to your favorites.

Marcia Jeans' SMART Board Web Sites

http://delicious.com/mjeans/smartboard

delicious   Home   Bookmarks ▼   People ▼

Marcia Jeans's smartboard **Bookmarks**

Yes, that is me, the author of this book. I am always looking for great Web sites that will help educators use their SMART Board more effectively. Check out my collection of sites!

Harvey's Homepage

http://harveyshomepage.com/Harveys_Homepage/Welcome.html

If you teach math in grades kindergarten through 8th grade, this is the site for you. It is loaded with creative, top-quality math Notebook lessons you can download for free.